THE ALL SPORTS PUZZLE AND QUIZ BOOK

GEORGE SULLIVAN

SCHOLASTIC BOOK SERVICES
New York Toronto London Auckland Sydney Tokyo

Cover photos/boxing: Focus on Sports; all others: Anthony Neste

ISBN: 0-590-30363-5

12 11 10 9 8 7 6 5 4 3 2 1 2 0 1 2 3 4 5/8

Printed in the U.S.A. 11

THE ALL SPORTS PUZZLE AND QUIZ BOOK

1 Match 'Em Up

Can you match the names of the performers in the lefthand column with the sport in which each competes?

1.	Tracy Austin	A.	Figure Skating
2.	Bert Jones	B.	Boxing
3.	Jim Rice	C.	Tennis
4.	Joan Joyce	D.	Ice Hockey
5.	Dorothy Hamill	E.	Softball
6.	Sugar Ray Leonard	F.	Gymnastics
		G.	Football
7.	Houston McTear	H.	Basketball
		I.	Horse Racing
8.	Giorgio Chinaglia	J.	Track
		K.	Bowling
9.	Suzy Chafee	L.	Baseball
10.	Dick Weber	M.	Soccer
11.	Nancy Lopez	N.	Hotdog Skiing
12.	Bill Walton	O.	Golf
13.	Kurt Thomas		
14.	Ron Franklin		
15.	Phil Esposito		

2 Hidden Words

The words given below may look like a rundown of the animals at your local zoo. Actually, they're the nicknames of teams in professional sports. How many of the names can you find. Some are spelled forward or backward; others up or down; and still others, diagonally.

Colts
Broncos
Bears
Eagles
Cubs
Orioles
Bruins
Toros
Bucks
Dolphins
Tigers
Rams
Bengals
Cardinals
Caribous
Penguins
Cougars
Sharks

D	O	L	P	H	I	N	S	M	A	R
B	B	O	S	O	C	N	O	R	B	S
S	E	S	S	T	I	G	E	R	S	L
T	A	N	L	U	S	C	U	B	S	A
L	R	S	G	H	O	I	O	R	S	N
O	S	N	A	A	N	B	A	T	E	I
C	E	R	O	S	L	G	I	O	L	D
P	K	N	I	L	U	S	S	R	G	R
S	S	E	L	O	I	R	O	O	A	A
N	B	U	C	K	S	O	L	S	E	C

3 What's the Sport?

This quiz tests your ability to recognize eight sports that aren't very well known. It's not likely you'll be able to identify them all, but get six right and you'll earn a passing grade.

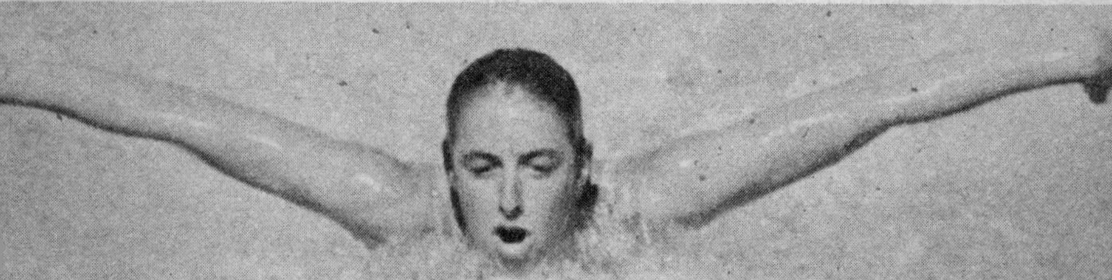

1. If you're a swimmer, you're likely to know this stroke to be the:

A. Butterfly
B. Side stroke
C. Crawl

2. Played outdoors in the East on fall and winter afternoons, this is:

A. Squash tennis
B. Racquet ball
C. Platform tennis

U.S. Forest Service

3. This young skiing competitor is involved in:

A. Downhill racing
B. Slalom racing
C. Cross country skiing

4. Not for sissies, this is:

A. Judo
B. Wrestling
C. Karate

Harness Racing Hall of Fame

5. This is Billy Boyce, a famous horse of the 1860s. Is Billy a:

A. Trotter
B. Pacer

6. Well-known to track and field enthusiasts, this event is the:

A. Shot put
B. Hammer throw
C. Discus throw

7. This young woman is lining up a shot in:

A. Pool
B. Billiards

8. The long bladed-skates are the tipoff. The sport is:

A. Dance skating
B. Figure skating
C. Speed skating

4 At the Supermarket

Pickles and peppers, apples and jam are not just terms from somebody's shopping list. They're also common to the sport of baseball. How many of the words from the column on the left can you correctly match with the definitions on the right?

1. can of corn
2. bagel job
3. hotdog
4. apple
5. pickle
6. rhubarb
7. jam
8. pepper
9. grapefruit league

A. to pitch inside, close to the hands
B. a showoff
C. teams that train in Florida
D. a high fly ball, easy to catch
E. a shutout
F. the baseball
G. warm-up drill
H. a dispute
I. a run-down play

5 Playing Around

The word "play" makes up part of each one of the terms you need to complete this quiz. How many can you get?

1. "Play __ __ __ __!" the umpire shouts to signal the beginning of a baseball game.

2. An error is a __ __ __ play.

3. In ice hockey, when one team has more players than another, a __ __ __ __ __ play results.

4. The player in hockey or basketball who spearheads his team's attack is known as a play__ __ __ __ __.

5. A play__ __ __ is an extra contest or a series of contests to determine a winner in the case of a tie or at the end of the regular season.

6. The runner on third base breaks for home, while the batter attempts to bunt the ball; it's a __ __ __ __ __ __ __ play.

7. When one party of golfers moves ahead of a slower party, they're said to be playing __ __ __ __ __ __ __.

8. A player who shows off to please the fans is guilty of a __ __ __ __ __ __ __ __ __ __ play.

6 Ball Game

This quiz tests your knowledge of the round objects that are thrown, kicked, dribbled, hit, or rolled in various games. Simply choose which ball is bigger.

1. A baseball or a softball?
2. A croquet ball or a tennis ball?
3. A volleyball or a soccer ball?
4. A volleyball or a basketball?
5. A tennis ball or a baseball?
6. A Ping-Pong ball or a golf ball?

7 You Can't Do That!

If you play soccer, you know that you're not allowed to either push or kick an opponent. This word-search puzzle is made up of words which describe rule violations common to various sports. How many of them can you find?

Push	**Bean**
Hold	**Shove**
Kick	**Travel**
Charge	**Strike**
Hack	**Wrestle**
Fight	**Balk**
Knee	**Punch**
Trip	**Chuck**
Obstruct	**Hit**

```
S H S U P F S T D K
T E H U K H I K L C
S R N I O I C G O A
C C A V T H C T H H
H T E V A E U K S T
U N W R E S T L E R
C A G N E L S A K I
K E K I R T S B T P
S B T C U R T S B O
```

8 Gone Hollywood

Many athletes have used sports as a stepping stone to the entertainment business. How many of these former sports stars can you identify?

1. A former lineman for the Detroit Lions, and a onetime commentator on television's *Monday Night Football,* he played the part of Mongo in the popular *Blazing Saddles.*

2. One of Hollywood's all-time greats, an Oscar winner in 1969 for his performance in *True Grit,* he starred in football for the University of Southern California.

3. A former running back, this man holds many of pro football's rushing records. He played the leading role in more than a dozen adventure films during the 1970s.

4. From Brooklyn, he played very briefly for the old Dodgers and also the Chicago Cubs. His lifetime batting average is .238. He's done much better in motion pictures and television.

5. Although he was a star quarterback for the New York Jets for almost 10 years, as a motion picture performer (he's pictured here in a scene from *C.C. and Company*) he was thrown for a loss on several occasions.

6. *Smokey and the Bandit* was one of the most successful films of the 1970s. His success as an actor has almost completely overshadowed the fact he once was a fine quarterback for Florida State University.

9 Home Grounds

Yankee Stadium is the home park for which major league baseball team? That's something like asking who's buried in Grant's tomb. But some of the other major-league stadiums are not as easy to identify as Yankee Stadium. Fifteen are listed below. Match 'em up.

1. Fenway Park	**A.** Chicago White Sox
2. Wrigley Field	**B.** Philadelphia Phillies
3. Memorial Stadium	**C.** Montreal Expos
4. Shea Stadium	**D.** Cleveland Indians
5. Riverfront Stadium	**E.** New York Mets
6. Olympic Stadium	**F.** Texas Rangers
7. Anaheim Stadium	**G.** Boston Red Sox
8. Comiskey Park	**H.** California Angels
9. Three Rivers Stadium	**I.** Cincinnati Reds
10. Veterans Stadium	**J.** Minnesota Twins
11. Candlestick Park	**K.** Chicago Cubs
12. Municipal Stadium	**L.** Pittsburgh Pirates
13. County Stadium	**M.** Baltimore Orioles
14. Metropolitan Stadium	**N.** Milwaukee Brewers
15. Arlington Stadium	**O.** San Francisco Giants

10 Fact or Fantasy?

Some of the statements in this quiz are true, while others are made up. Can you spot the fakes?

1. The shortest player in major-league history was a midget 42 inches in height. His name was Eddie Gaedel and he played for the St. Louis Browns in a game against the Detroit Tigers on August 19, 1951.

2. Some referees in the National Hockey League did not begin using whistles until the 1930s. Instead, they carried small bells which they tinkled at offenders.

3. On August 18, 1974, Abla Khairi of Egypt became the youngest person to swim the English Channel, making the crossing from Cap Griz Nez in France to Dover, England, in 12 hours, 30 minutes. He was 13 years old at the time.

4. Hockey sticks can be either "righthanded" or "left-handed."

5. International soccer competition was launched in 1930, with nations competing for the World Cup. In the 13 World Cup tournaments that have been held since that time, the English have proven the game's masters, winning four times.

6. Mickey Mantle of the New York Yankees, who retired in 1968, rates as one of baseball's greatest switch hitters. Ten times during his career he hit home runs from both sides of the plate during a game.

7. Although the Soviet Union did not enter Olympic competiton until 1952, that nation now leads all others in terms of gold medals won.

8. The practice of having the President of the United States toss out a ball to open the baseball season was begun by Harry S Truman, when, on April 10, 1946, he threw out a baseball before the game between the Washington Senators and Boston Red Sox.

9. No player who ever won the Heisman Trophy, awarded annually to the best college player, has ever been elected to the Pro Football Hall of Fame.

10. The New York Yankees have never finished in last place in the American League.

11. Bruce Jenner was one of America's heroes in the 1976 Olympic Games, winning a gold medal in the decathlon competition. It marked the first time an American had ever won the event.

12. The Chicago Sting of the North American Soccer League once had a midfielder named Richie Duda whose nickname was Zippity.

11 Scrambled Teams

Each of the jumbled words below is the name of a city with a major league baseball team. Can you un-jumble them?

1. T E A S E L T
2. T I M B E R L A O
3. H P I G T R S U B T
4. T O B N O S
5. G H C I O C A
6. K L M E A I U E W
7. D I P L H A L I E P A H
8. L E A M N O T R
9. D A L E E N L V C
10. N U O H T S O

12 For the Famous

Not long ago, officials of the sport of soaring, an activity that involves piloting a sailplane for long periods of time, established a Soaring Hall of Fame in Frankfort, Michigan. You probably didn't know that. But the location of several other Halls of Fame you surely do know. See how many Halls and locations you can link up from the lists below.

1. National Professional Football Hall of Fame
2. Hockey Hall of Fame
3. Naismith Memorial Basketball Hall of Fame
4. National Ski Hall of Fame
5. National Baseball Museum and Hall of Fame
6. International Swimming Hall of Fame
7. International Lawn Tennis Hall of Fame and Museum

A. Ishpeming, Michigan
B. Newport, Rhode Island
C. Canton, Ohio
D. Ft. Lauderdale, Florida
E. Toronto, Ontario
F. Springfield, Massachusetts
G. Cooperstown, New York

13 Symbol Quiz

In 1948, Fred Gehrke, a halfback for the Los Angeles Rams, painted yellow horns on his team's blue leather helmet. That started a trend. In the years that followed, other National Football League teams began applying monograms and identifying symbols to their helmets. The pictures of 10 of them are presented on these pages. Number 1 is the Rams' symbol. How many others can you identify?

1.

2.

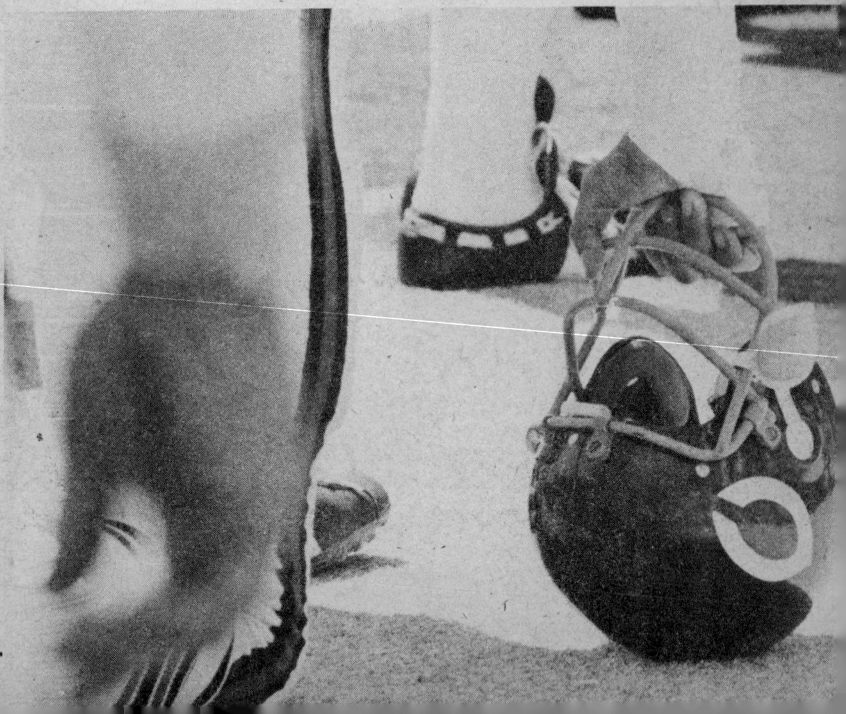

3.

5.

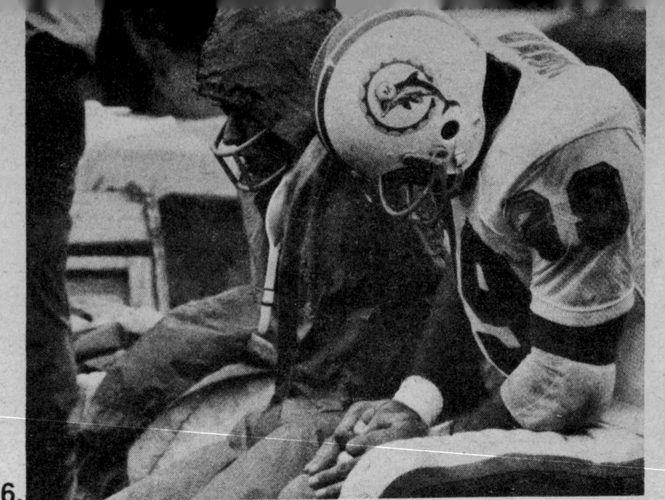

6.

7.

9.

10.

14 Sports Galore

The names of almost two dozen sports played in the United States are listed below. Find as many of them as you can by looking forward, backward, or diagonally.

Billiards	**Polo**
Bowling	**Skating**
Boxing	**Rowing**
Croquet	**Sailing**
Darts	**Skeet**
Diving	**Skiing**
Golf	**Soccer**
Handball	**Squash**
Hiking	**Tennis**
Karting	**Track**
Lacrosse	**Wrestling**

F G S F S A I L I N G A
L E K K S K A T I N G S
O L E A G C S A N N I E
G E S P R A G N I V I D
T H O O S T S K I I N G
R L S A R O I E S G R N
O S O A S H G N I N T I
E O C G U A S N G I E L
S K C S N Q E A I L U T
S T E N N I S G I W Q S
S D R A I L L I B O O E
E A S A G N I X O B R R
L L A B D N A H A S C W

15 Nicknames—1

It's well-known that Orenthal James Simpson, perhaps football's flashiest performer of the 1970s, was nicknamed "The Juice." Other famous nicknames are listed in the column on the left. "Real" names are on the right. You should be able to match all but two or three, if you know your players.

1. The Louisville Lip
2. Yaz
3. Pelé
4. Catfish
5. The Eraser
6. The Kid
7. The Bird
8. Tiny
9. The Penguin
10. The Pearl
11. Broadway Joe
12. The Big E

A. Carl Yastrzemski
B. Ron Cey
C. Muhammad Ali
D. Earl Monroe
E. Steve Cauthen
F. Elvin Hayes
G. Jim Hunter
H. Edson Arantes do Nascimento
I. Joe Namath
J. Mark Fidrych
K. Nate Archibald
L. Marvin Webster

16 Nicknames—2

This is a bit more difficult. It's based on nicknames of sports stars of the past. If you get stuck, ask someone older for help.

1. The Stilt	**A.** Jay Hanna Dean
2. Red	**B.** Maureen Connolly
3. Whitey	**C.** Rocco Barbella
4. Rocky Graziano	**D.** Wilt Chamberlain
5. The Brown Bomber	**E.** Edwin Ford
6. Lefty	**F.** Maurice Richard
7. The Rocket	**G.** Bernie Geoffrion
8. Little Mo	**H.** Harold Grange
9. Joltin' Joe	**I.** Leo Durocher
10. Leo the Lip	**J.** Joe Louis
11. Dizzy	**K.** Robert Moses Grove
12. Boom Boom	**L.** Joe DiMaggio

17 Olympic Sites

The Olympic Games were staged in Los Angeles in 1932, and will be there again in 1984. Some of the other cities that have hosted Olympic competition are listed below. Find as many as you can in the puzzle diagram. They're all there.

Athens	Helsinki
Paris	Melbourne
London	Rome
Stockholm	Tokyo
Antwerp	Munich
Amsterdam	Montreal
Berlin	Moscow

T	L	A	E	R	T	N	O	M	S	O
S	P	R	E	W	T	N	A	R	M	E
B	P	K	I	O	E	D	O	D	E	S
I	K	A	Y	E	R	M	M	B	N	H
M	O	K	R	E	S	U	O	E	R	E
W	O	O	T	I	N	S	H	R	U	L
T	H	S	M	I	S	T	I	L	O	S
M	M	W	C	L	A	S	E	I	B	I
A	S	H	L	O	N	D	O	N	L	N
H	M	P	N	R	W	O	U	S	E	K
I	S	T	O	C	K	H	O	L	M	I

18 Weighty Problems

Which is heavier?

1. A bowling ball or a bowling pin?
2. A football or a basketball?
3. A softball or a baseball?
4. A golf ball or a tennis ball?
5. A soccer ball or a volleyball?

19 What's My Name?

A handful of the best known athletes of all time are described and pictured on these pages. How many can you identify?

Pro Football Hall of Fame

1. In 1950, to mark the mid-century, the nation's sportswriters were polled to determine the name of the athlete they believed to be the "greatest of all time"—and they named me. I was born on an Indian reservation in Oklahoma, a member of the Sac and Fox tribe. I was a college football star at Carlisle University, won the pentathlon and decathlon in the 1912 Olympic Games (five events in one, ten in the other), and played major-league baseball and professional football. There was no sport I could not play, and play well. I am ________.

CBS-TV Sports

2. I was born in the Soviet Union. My career in gymnastics began in 1964 when I was nine. The sport became the most important thing in my life. At the 1972 Olympic Games in Munich, I won individual gold medals in floor exercise and the beam competition. The crowds loved me. But at the 1976 Olympics, I had to be content with merely a silver medal. Nevertheless, many people say that I did more than any other performer to help make gymnastics the popular sport it is today. I am ________.

New York Public Library

3. Beginning with the season of 1925 and continuing until 1939, I played in 2,130 consecutive games for the New York Yankees, a record that has been called "incredible." It's not likely to ever be broken. I hit 493 home runs and had a career batting average of .340. Yet often I was overshadowed by a teammate of mine, the great slugger Babe Ruth (pictured on my right in this photo). My name is ________.

4. When I was 15 years old, I already stood 6-foot-10. I stopped growing when I reached 7-foot-2. Basketball was my sport — naturally. I was a high school sensation and college superstar. As a professional, I once scored 100 points in a game. Another time, I had 78 points. I averaged 30.1 points per game during my career. Although about a decade has passed since I retired, most of pro basketball's individual scoring records are still mine. Who am I?

____

FOOT
BALL
Program

—

December
25th, 1925

—

CORAL
GABLES
FLA.

National Baseball Hall of Fame

5. As a schoolboy in Wheaton, Illinois, I won 16 letters in various sports. As a college football player, I set records that have never been equaled. In one game, I handled the ball five times and scored four touchdowns. They called me the "Galloping Ghost." As a pro player for the Chicago Bears, huge crowds turned out to see me play. Sportswriters have said that I "put pro football on the map." Name me. ________

20 Sports-Minded Presidents

American Presidents have frequently taken refuge from the pressures of their work in athletic exercises of one type or another. Indeed, Dwight D. Eisenhower, during his two terms as President, spent so much time on the golf course that he was frequently the butt of good-natured jokes. This quiz concerns these Presidents:

Jimmy Carter
Richard Nixon
Gerald Ford
John F. Kennedy
Franklin Roosevelt
Theodore Roosevelt

How many of them can you identify from these descriptions?

1. Although the victim of infantile paralysis and an invalid, this President swam and sailed. In his youth, he skied and golfed, and, as a college student at Harvard, he rowed.

2. This President, like Eisenhower, was also a golfer, but not a very good one. He once struck a spectator as he was driving from a tee. He was more noted for his achievements as a college football player. A center, he was the captain of his team at the University of Michigan.

3. Pictures of this President jogging about the White House grounds were often seen in newspapers and magazines during the late 1970s. He was a stock-car racing fan and, as a high school student, he played baseball. On vacations, he sometimes played softball.

4. This President was a bench-warmer on his college football team. During his presidency, he once referred to himself as the "nation's No. 1 football fan." In 1972, he suggested a play to Miami coach Don Shula just before the Super Bowl. He was a baseball fan, too. Once retired, he played golf occasionally.

5. History books sometimes picture this President astride a horse, leading American "Rough Riders" as a lieutenant-colonel in the Spanish-American War. Besides being a skilled rider, he also played baseball, football, and tennis. He boxed, rowed, and was a noted big-game hunter. He has been called the best athlete to have served as President.

6. Swimming and sailing in the waters near his Hyannis Port, Massachusetts, home were among this President's favorite sports. He also enjoyed golf and tennis. Until he injured his back, he was an enthusiastic participant in his family's touch football games.

21 Flying Baseballs

The sky is filled with baseballs. You have to pick out one to catch. But first separate each ball from the others by drawing **only three pairs of parallel lines.**

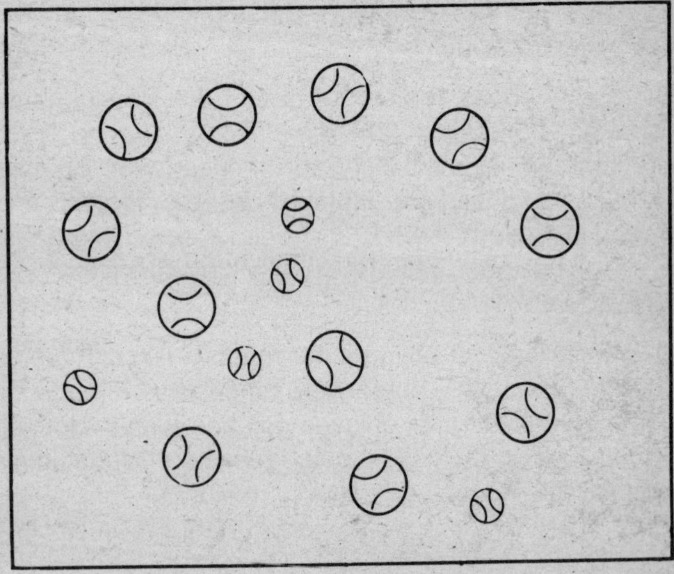

22 Calendar Quiz

The idea here is to arrange the six events listed below in their proper sequence; the earliest event is to be listed first, the next earliest, second, etc. Good luck!

A. The American Basketball Association comes into existence, challenging the National Basketball Association.

B. Eight members of the Chicago White Sox "sell out" to gamblers before the World Series.

C. Roger Maris hits 61 home runs for the season.

D. Roger Bannister becomes the first runner in history to break the 4-minute mark in the mile run.

E. Swimmer Mark Spitz returns from the Olympic Games in Munich with a record seven gold medals.

F. Jesse Owens, winning gold medals in the 100-meter and 200-meter dashes, creates a sensation at the Berlin Olympics.

23 Skiing Talk

There's more to skiing than boots, poles, and the skis themselves — as this hidden-word quiz suggests. How many of the skiing terms can you find?

Alpine	**Hairpin**
Bail	**Mogul**
Base	**Swing**
Binding	**Shovel**
Boot	**Slalom**
Camber	**Slope**
Check	**Tail**
Pole	**Tip**
Ski	**Touring**
Track	**Tuck**

B	D	T	O	U	R	I	N	G	L
A	M	S	L	E	D	G	L	T	U
S	O	T	B	I	N	D	I	N	G
E	L	M	S	I	P	H	A	B	O
S	A	B	W	T	O	O	B	L	M
C	L	S	E	N	I	P	L	A	T
H	S	H	O	V	E	L	A	E	P
E	T	L	H	A	I	R	P	I	N
C	I	K	C	A	R	T	T	K	I
K	C	U	T	E	P	O	L	S	T

24 When?

Because it's always played in October, the World Series is sometimes called the "fall classic." How many other championship sporting events, listed in the column on the left, can you match up with the appropriate month?

1. U.S. Tennis Open, Flushing Meadow
2. U.S. Golf Open
3. Soccer Bowl
4. Rose Bowl
5. Kentucky Derby
6. Baseball All-Star Game

A. May
B. July
C. September
D. June
E. August
F. January

25 Kid Stuff

Two or three times a year, newspaper headlines proclaim the feats of sports heroes who are noted as much for their youth as for what they achieved. This quiz concerns some of these young champions and their remarkable accomplishments.

1. Name the youngest individual ever to play major league baseball.

A. Joe Nuxhall
B. Pete Rose
C. Ted Williams

2. In 1975, a member of the Boston Red Sox became the youngest player in baseball history to win a Most Valuable Player award. What was his name?

A. Jim Rice
B. Carlton Fisk
C. Fred Lynn

3. Who was the youngest player to win a batting title?

A. Al Kaline
B. Willie Mays
C. Rod Carew

4. In 1977, a 16-year-old jockey, nicknamed "The Kid," won 487 races and was named "Male Athlete of the Year." Name him.

A. Angel Cordero
B. Jorge Velasquez
C. Steve Cauthen

5. One of baseball's greatest sluggers was also known as "The Kid." With a .406 batting in 1941, he stands as the last player to hit more than .400 for a season. His name is:

A. Jimmy Foxx
B. Joe Cronin
C. Ted Williams

6. How many high school athletes have run the mile in less than four minutes.

A. 3
B. 13
C. 44

7. Name the youngest person to ever appear on the cover of *Sports Illustrated* Magazine.

A. Tracy Austin
B. Steve Cauthen
C. Nadia Comaneci

8. Johnny Miles of Sydney Mines, Nova Scotia, was the youngest runner ever to win the Boston Marathon. He accomplished the feat in 1926. How old was he?

A. 7 years old
B. 16 years old
C. 20 years old

9. Five-year-old Bucky Cox of Lawrence, Kansas, set a record for children under the age of six in the marathon (26 miles, 385 yards) in 1977. What was Bucky's time for the distance?

A. 3 hours, 48 minutes, 11 seconds
B. 5 hours, 25 minutes, 9 seconds
C. 6 hours, 35 minutes, 48 seconds

10. A Brooklyn, New York, schoolgirl dominated women's pocket billiards throughout the 1970s, winning her first national championship in 1971 at the age of 13. Name her.

A. Gloria Walker
B. Jean Balukas
C. Billie Billing

26 Spelling Bee

Which of the terms below have been spelled incorrectly? A clue: There are six of them.

1. javelen
2. referee
3. mit
4. aparatus
5. barrell
6. bogey
7. canoe
8. toboggon
9. croquet
10. scissors
11. duece
12. lacrosse
13. karate
14. neutral zone

27 Sneaking Out

It wasn't very many years ago that the most popular sports shoe was the sneaker. Well, just plain sneakers have gone the way of the hoop skirt. Sports footwear is highly specialized today. How many different sports can you identify from the shoes pictured on these pages? You should be able to get at least six.

1. Football players and basketball players once wore high-topped shoes. Not any more. Now they're common to only one sport. It's _ _ _ _ _ _.

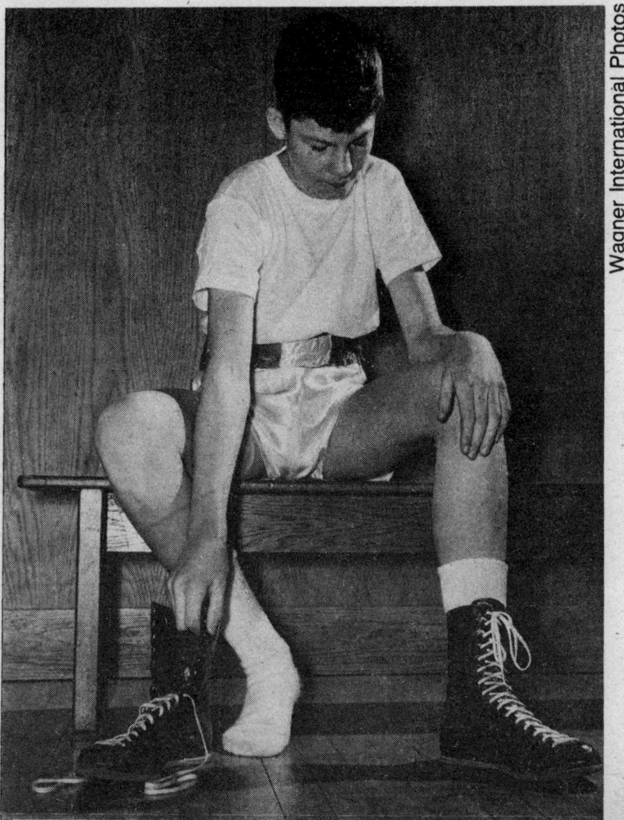

Wagner International Photos

2. If the rounded cleats don't tip off what this sport is, the ball surely will. It's _ _ _ _ _ _.

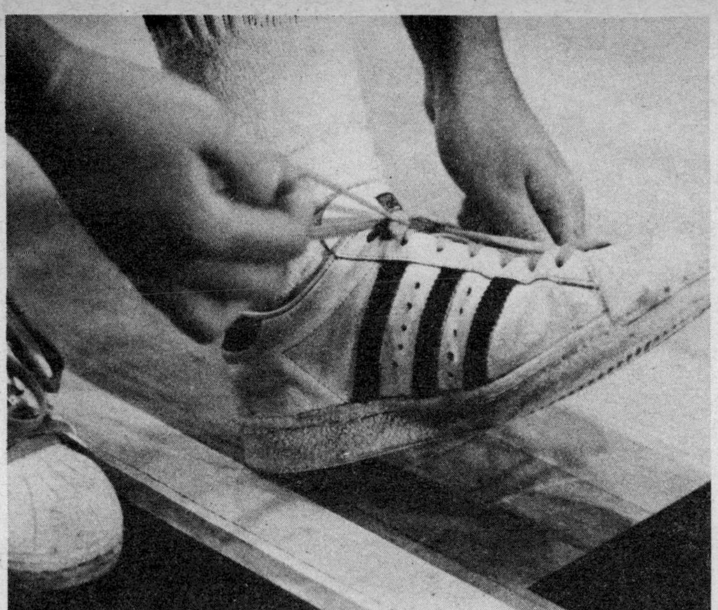

3. Light in weight, with nylon uppers and non-skid treads, you wear these in _ _ _ _ _ _ _ _ _ _ _ _ _ _.

National Park Service

4. Put these on and you're off for a day of _ _ _ _ _ _ _.

5. Shoes with laces on the sides? Why would that be important? The sport is __ __ __ __ __ __ __ __.

6. The fact that the shoe in the foreground is square-tipped is the clue to the sport involved. It's _ _ _ _ _ _ _ _.

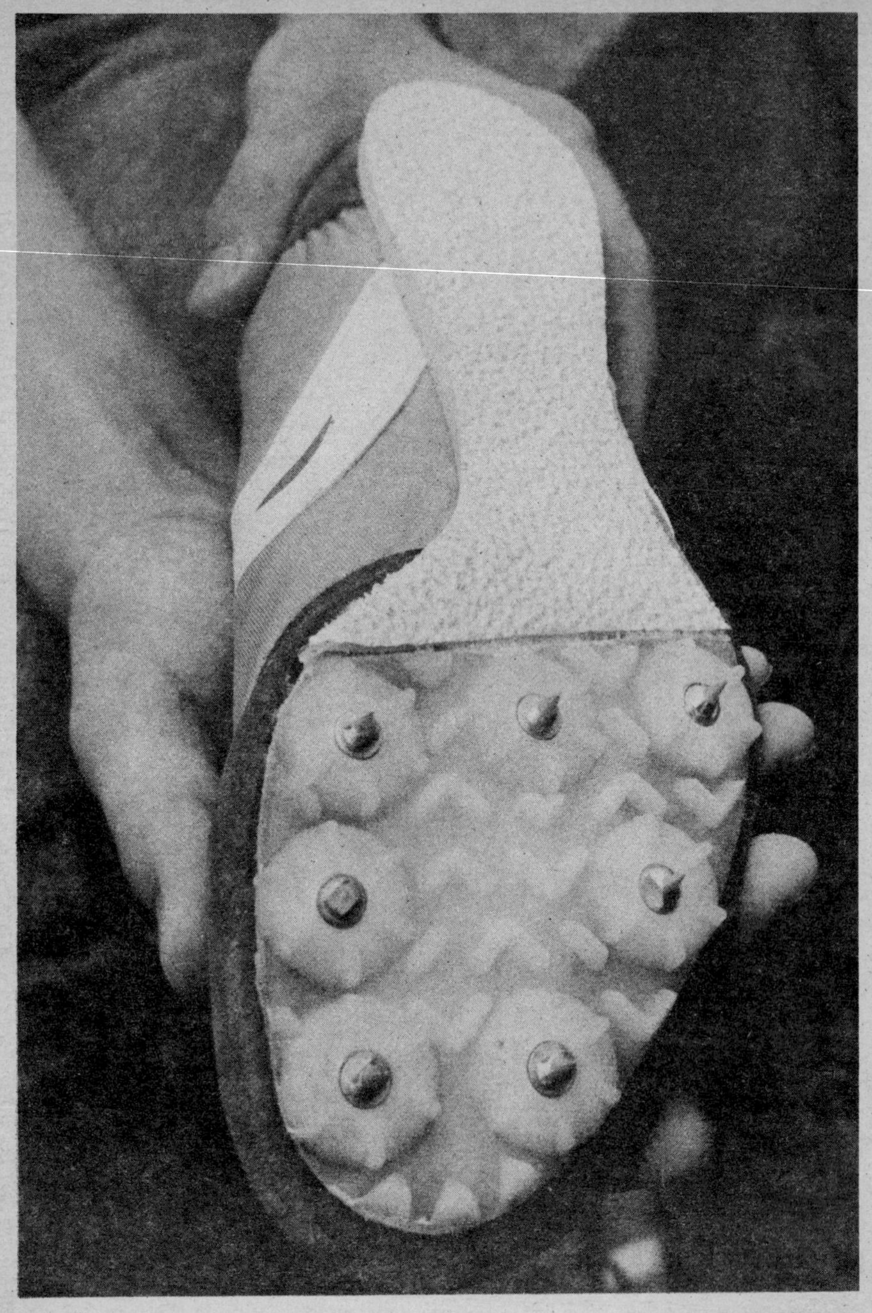

7. These are called spikes, but they surely aren't meant for baseball. The sport is __ __ __ __ __.

8. Notice the cushioning and the distinctive tread. These are for _ _ _ _ _ _ _.

28 In Reverse

This is a different kind of a quiz. Instead of being asked questions, you're given the answers. It's up to you to supply the questions for each. All concern the sport of baseball. You should be able to get at least six of them. But watch out, a couple are very tricky.

1. "The House That Ruth Built"
2. 162 games
3. 56 games
4. May 24, 1935
5. 755 homers
6. 1903
7. 84,587 fans
8. \$7½ million
9. The first team to win four games
10. Strike

29 Double-Letter Words

The terms in this word list have three things in common: They're all sports terms, they all contain a double letter, and they're all hidden.

Arrow
Barrel
Error
Freeze
Gallery
Gallop
Juggle
Leeward
Scissors
Paddle
Screen
Keel
Pennant
Rally
Putt
Offense
Skittles
Snooker
Troll
Lacrosse

E T R R N P Y L L A R L
L E E K O P E N N A N T
G A L L E R Y R P U T T
E P L R R E R R O R R E
L A T A E A A E G O L S
G D B L C N R R L E R N
G D E E E R O L R O L E
U L R E K O O N S O R F
J E R W M R R S E L W F
L C A A R R I E S T T O
S E E R R C E Z E E R F
E R R D S E L T T I K S

30 Notable Quotes

"Nice guys finish last," a major league manager said many years ago, but the phrase remains in widespread use to this day. How many of these quotations can you complete?

1. "Good _ _ _ _ _, no hit."
2. "Hit 'em where they _ _ _ _ _."
3. "A punt, a pass, and a _ _ _ _ _ _."
4. "Playing a tie game is like _ _ _ _ _ _ _   _ _ _ _   _ _ _ _ _ _."
5. "When the going gets tough, the tough _ _ _   _ _ _ _ _."
6. "_ _ _ _ _ _ _ is the only thing."
7. "It's not whether you win or lose, it's _ _ _   _ _ _   _ _ _ _   _ _ _   _ _ _ _."
8. "We play them _ _ _   _ _ _ _   _ _   _   _ _ _ _."
9. "Float like a _ _ _ _ _ _ _ _ _, sting like a _ _ _."
10. "The opera ain't over till _ _ _   _ _ _   _ _ _ _   _ _ _ _ _."

31 Specialists

When two football teams line up for the snap of the ball, one squad's offensive team faces the other squad's defensive team, and each player is assigned a specific role to play. From the standard abbreviations shown here, how many positions can you identify?

Defensive Team

S ______________________________

CB ______________________________

LB ______________________________

DT ______________________________

DE ______________________________

Offensive Team

W ______________________________

OG ______________________________

OT ______________________________

C ______________________________

TE ______________________________

Q ______________________________

RB ______________________________

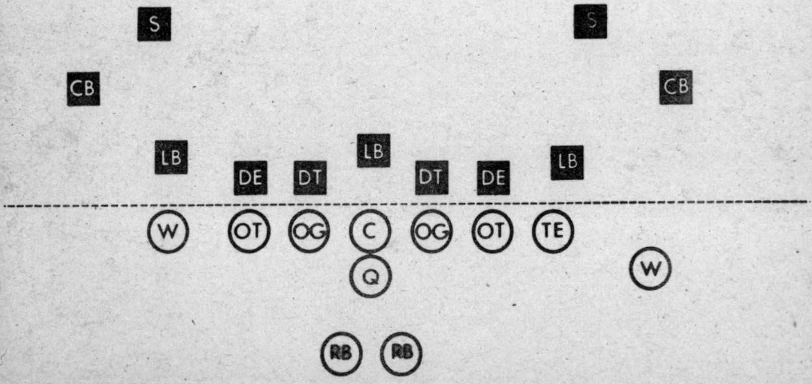

32 For Short

Many leagues and sports organizations are frequently referred to by their initials rather than by their complete names. How many of the below listed abbreviations do you know?

1. N.F.L.
2. A.F.C.
3. N.B.A.
4. N.A.S.L.
5. N.C.A.A.
6. N.H.L.
7. P.G.A.
8. U.S.T.A.
9. A.A.U.
10. N.I.T.
11. A.I.A.W.
12. N.R.A.

33 What's the Score

Everyone knows that the basic scoring unit in baseball is the run, registered each time a base runner reaches home plate safely. But in some other sports, the scoring terms are less well known. A number of them are listed in the left-hand column, while the sports they refer to are listed on the right. How many can you match?

1. Takedown	**A.** Football
2. Rouge	**B.** Golf
3. Free throw	**C.** Bowling
4. Touch	**D.** Canadian football
5. Stroke	**E.** Wrestling
6. Pins	**F.** Billiards
7. Safety	**G.** Rugby
8. Ringer	**H.** Fencing
9. Try	**I.** Basketball
10. Cannon	**J.** Horseshoe pitching

34 Women Athletes

Here's a quiz that tests your knowledge of some of the leading figures in women's sports, past and present. Can you identify at least six of them.

1. Who was the young Romanian woman who dominated gymnastics competition in the 1976 Olympic Games, winning four gold medals?

A. Karin Janz
B. Teodora Ungureanu
C. Nadia Comaneci

2. In the same Olympics, another competitor, a representative of the Soviet Union, captured three golds in women's gymnastics. Name her.

A. Ludmila Turischeva
B. Olga Korbut
C. Nelli Kim

3. Madison Square Garden's all-time individual scoring record in basketball is held—not by Kareem Abdul-Jabbar or Wilt Chamberlain — but by a woman. She played for Montclair (New Jersey) State College and scored 52 points against Queens College in 1977. Her name:

A. Carol Blazejowski
B. Donna Sims
C. Nancy Lieberman

4. What woman made history in 1967 by entering the Boston Marathon dressed as a man.

A. Miki Gorman
B. Nina Kuscsik
C. Kathy Switzer

5. When this woman was 15, she became the youngest in tennis history to reach the semifinals in the U.S. Open. At 21, she earned more money than any player—male or female—had ever won in a single year. Name her.

A. Chris Evert
B. Billie Jean King
C. Maureen Connolly

6. What woman dominated pocket billiards during the 1970s, winning eight consecutive championships?

A. Gloria Walker
B. Jean Balukas
C. Billie Billing

7. *Swimming World* Magazine called her "probably the greatest female swimmer ever." Only 17 when she competed in the 1976 Olympics, she won four gold medals and one silver. What was her name?

A. Kornelia Ender
B. Andrea Pollack
C. Shirley Babashoff

8. During the late 1970s, UCLA frequently dominated women's basketball. Star of the team and "Player of the Year" in the sport in 1979 was:

A. Lucie Harris
B. Ann Meyers
C. Anita Ortega

9. What woman is the only sprinter—male or female—to win a gold medal for the 100-meter dash in two different Olympics?

A. Wyomia Tyus
B. Barbara Ferrell
C. Helen Stephens

35 Well-Equipped

Jib is a sailing term. It's the word used to describe the triangular sail set forward of the boat's mast. A sinker is a lead weight you attach to a fishing line to keep it below the surface. See how many other pieces of equipment you can find in the puzzle diagram.

Sinker	Jib	Club	Rack
Ski	Tank	Racket	Bridle
Grip	Dart	Stick	Halter
Jig	Oar	Arrow	Target
Tee	Backpack	Skate	Mitt
Rope	Barbell	Goal	Mat
Mallet	Pin	Paddle	Saddle

```
J I B L G S T I C K
L P K P I N E L P C
L I L N J O U B I A
E T K C A B A K R P
B E O S P T T R P K
R L S L E H O O I C
A D N K I W E P R A
B D C C A B L E G B
C A K A H T S P T R
R P I R R A E E A I
O T R A D E L C R D
T A M D K L L T G L
O J L O A G K B E E
A E N M I T T P T R
```

36 Baseball's Best

Being elected to baseball's Hall of Fame is the greatest honor a player can receive. Out of the many thousands of players who have appeared in the major leagues since 1871, only 200 have become Hall of Famers. The photographs of eight of the most noted Hall of Fame members appear on these pages. Their names and the year each was admitted to Hall of Fame membership are printed below. How many photos and names can you match?

Babe Ruth—1936 ______________________
Ty Cobb—1936 ______________________
Mel Ott—1951 ______________________
Satchel Paige—1971 ______________________
Yogi Berra—1972 ______________________
Mickey Mantle—1974 ______________________
Ralph Kiner—1975 ______________________
Willie Mays—1979 ______________________

1.

National Baseball Hall of Fame

2. National Baseball Hall of Far

3.

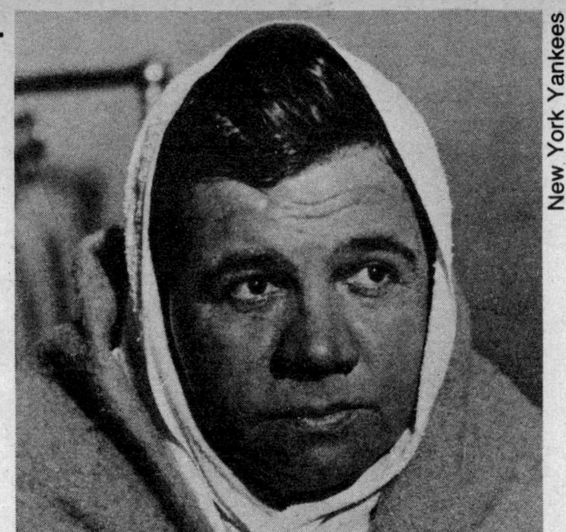

New York Yankees

4.

5.

6.

7.

8.

37 Tennis Anyone?

Tennis is truly an international sport. Players come from all over the world. The names of ten tennis stars are listed on the left, their native countries, on the right. How many can you match?

1. Bjorn Borg	**A.** Spain
2. Ilie Nastase	**B.** Soviet Union
3. Virginia Wade	**C.** Argentina
4. Martina Navratilova	**D.** Sweden
5. Manuel Orantes	**E.** Australia
6. Vitas Gerulaitis	**F.** Romania
7. Francoise Durr	**G.** Czechoslovakia
8. Olga Morozova	**H.** United States
9. Evonne Goolagong Cawley	**I.** France
10. Guillermo Vilas	**J.** Great Britain

38 For the Birds

Many college basketball teams are named after our fine feathered friends. How many of these "bird" nicknames only can you spot?

Blackbirds (Long Island University)
Owls (Temple University)
Cardinals (University of Louisville)
Eagles (Boston College)
Gamecocks (University of South Carolina)
Webfoots (University of Oregon)
Jayhawks (University of Iowa)
Peacocks (Saint Peter's College)
Griffins (Canisius College)
Gobblers (Virginia Polytechnic Institute)
Falcons (Bowling Green University)
Hawks (St. Joseph's College)

S	G	O	B	B	L	E	R	S	K	C	A
S	K	S	S	H	A	W	K	E	Y	E	S
N	F	C	B	N	O	C	I	K	S	A	T
I	I	C	D	C	O	G	S	K	F	G	O
F	P	E	A	C	O	C	K	S	S	L	O
F	S	C	E	R	H	I	L	K	S	E	F
I	C	M	S	A	D	W	K	A	O	S	B
R	A	I	W	K	O	I	C	S	F	M	E
G	C	K	C	S	I	K	N	B	O	J	W
S	S	D	R	I	B	K	C	A	L	B	C
H	I	C	S	F	K	P	S	Y	L	O	H
C	K	S	J	A	Y	H	A	W	K	S	F

39 Back Talk

Everyone knows that when you ride a horse without a saddle, you're riding bare*back*. How many of these other "back" terms to you know?

1. The screen or fence behind homeplate in the game of baseball is called a back __ __ __ __.

2. In basketball, the fan-shaped or rectangular surface to which the basket is attached is called a back__ __ __ __ __.

3. When a football player downs the ball in his own end zone, a __ __ __ __ __back is registered.

4. On a race track, the side opposite the finish line is called the back__ __ __ __ __ __ __.

5. A _ _ _ _ _back is a pitch that's thrown high and inside, forcing the batter to move away from the plate.

6. When a player gets out of a slump or recovers from an injury, he's made a _ _ _ _back.

7. A bowling ball that curves from left to right is termed back_ _ ball.

8. In football, the _ _ _ _ _ _ _backs are stationed between the safeties and the linebackers.

9. The second half of an 18-hole golf course is called the back _ _ _ _.

10. A basketball player cuts away from the man defending him, circles behind the other defensive players, then gets a quick pass beneath the basket. It's a back_ _ _ _ play.

11. The football players positioned behind the linemen are called the back_ _ _ _ _.

40 National Pastime

Baseball is said to be more popular today than at any time in the nation's history. If you're a fan of the sport, you should be able to get at least ten of these questions correct.

1. What player holds the major league record for strikeouts in a season?

A. Nolan Ryan
B. Sandy Koufax
C. Cy Young

2. Which team has won the most World Series?

3. Which team has opened at home more than any other?

4. Match these one-time baseball parks with the city in which each was located.

1. Braves Field	**A.** San Francisco
2. Griffith Stadium	**B.** New York
3. Polo Grounds	**C.** Boston
4. Seals Stadium	**D.** Washington

5. What baseball team was known as "The Big Red Machine"?

6. A player nicknamed "Charlie Hustle" once starred for that team and later played for the Philadelphia Phillies. Name him.

7. Who pitched a perfect game for the New York Yankees against the Brooklyn Dodgers in the 1956 World Series?

8. Which one of the following is not a major league baseball player?

A. Bob Horner
B. Craig Swan
C. Gary Maddox
D. Tony Dorsett

9. Who is the only player in major league history to win an MVP Award in each league?

10. Mickey Mantle is the all-time strikeout leader in major league baseball. He has a total of 1,710 whiffs. What player holds that distinction in the National League?

11. This player is more known for home runs than walks, but he holds the major league record for bases on balls.

A. Hank Aaron
B. Roger Maris
C. Babe Ruth

12. The Cy Young award is given annually to the best pitcher in each major league. A National League relief pitcher once won it. What was his name?

13. Which of these hitters failed to get 3,000 hits in his career?

A. Rogers Hornsby
B. Ty Cobb
C. Paul Waner

14. What is often regarded as the most noted home run in baseball history was struck by a native of Glasgow, Scotland, in 1951. He played for the New York Giants. Name him.

15. The last pitcher to win 30 games in a season turned the trick in 1968. He was a lefty, a member of the Detroit Tigers. His name is:

A. Mickey Lolich
B. Denny McLain
C. Early Wynn

41 Super Quiz

Most fans agree that the Super Bowl is the nation's No. 1 sports event. News coverage of the game fills the sports pages for weeks. As a television production, it is one of the most popular shows of the year, attracting almost 100 million viewers. Can you answer these "super" questions?

1. In what year was the Super Bowl first played?

A. 1912
B. 1947
C. 1967
D. 1955

2. The first team to win three Super Bowl games was the:

A. New York Jets
B. Oakland Raiders
C. Pittsburgh Steelers
D. Dallas Cowboys

3. Match the names of these Super Bowl stadiums with the cities in which each is located:

1. Orange Bowl	**A.** New Orleans, Louisiana
2. Rose Bowl	**B.** Miami, Florida
3. Tulane Stadium	**C.** Pasadena, California
4. Memorial Coliseum	**D.** Los Angeles, California
5. Rice Stadium	**E.** Houston, Texas

4. The "losingest" Super Bowl team is the:

A. New York Giants
B. Minnesota Vikings
C. Denver Broncos
D. Baltimore Colts

5. Name the coach that has participated in more Super Bowls than any other:

A. Tom Landry, Dallas Cowboys
B. Don Shula, Miami Dolphins
C. Bud Grant, Minnesota Vikings

6. The largest crowd in Super Bowl history watched the Raiders defeat the Vikings in 1977. How many people were on hand?

A. 110,702
B. 103,438
C. 97,623
D. 80,680

7. What is ranked as the greatest upset in Super Bowl history occurred in Super Bowl III. What happened?

8. Only one defensive player has won the Super Bowl's Most Valuable Player award. That happened in Super Bowl V. The player was:

A. Bob Lilly
B. Herb Adderley
C. Chuck Howley

42 Sports Movies

Scenes from recent Hollywood films which have a sports background are shown on these pages. How many of the films can you identify? You should be able to get them all. The films are:

Kansas City Bomber
Brian's Song
Rocky
Slap Shot
Semi-Tough
One on One

1. ______________________________

3. ______________________________

4. ______________________________

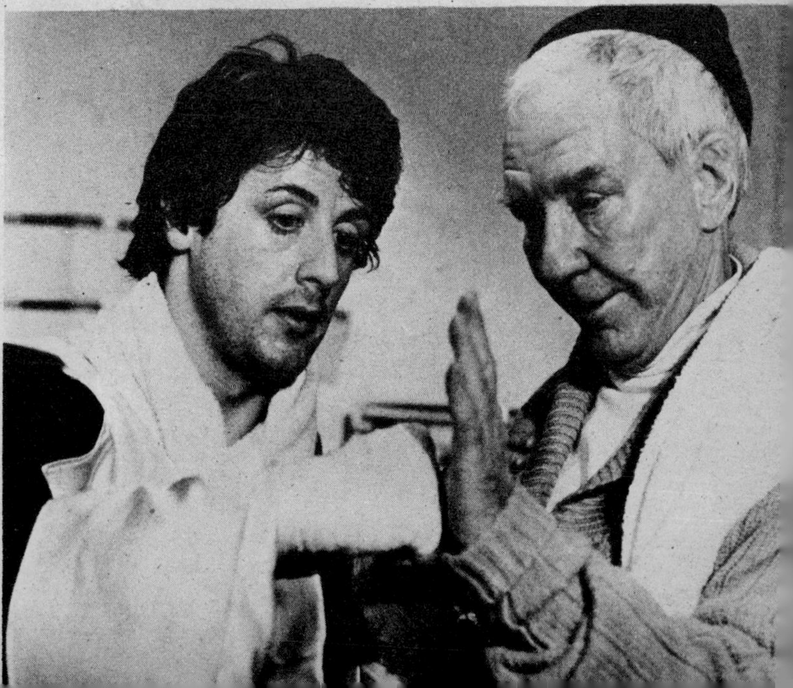

5. ______________________________

6. ______________________________

Movie Star News

43 Gone But Not Forgotten

Investing in professional football used to be very risky. This list contains the names of teams that were once active but no longer exist. Find the names in the puzzle diagram.

Wheels	**Wings**	**Blues**	**Gunners**
Sharks	**Stars**	**Kodaks**	**Reds**
Legions	**Stapletons**	**Badgers**	
Dodgers	**Steels**	**Texans**	
Indians	**Bisons**	**Pros**	

L	S	W	E	S	N	S	L	E	E	H	W
S	E	S	G	U	N	N	E	R	S	S	A
O	S	G	E	A	I	O	N	S	R	W	S
R	A	K	I	B	K	S	S	A	G	N	O
P	W	D	S	O	R	O	T	I	O	S	E
B	N	B	D	E	N	S	A	T	B	E	S
I	B	A	G	S	S	S	E	S	S	U	S
A	K	D	S	K	I	L	N	D	W	L	N
S	O	G	W	R	P	E	E	S	E	B	A
D	E	E	S	A	B	R	O	E	N	S	X
W	I	R	T	H	S	R	T	O	H	A	E
S	A	S	B	S	N	S	G	N	I	W	T

44 Going Metric

The changeover to the metric system has had a greater effect on track than any other sport, with more and more races being run over metric distances, rather than being described in feet and yards.

If you're a member of a track team, this quiz will be easy. If you're not—well, lots of luck. For each of the pairs of distances listed, simply tell which is the longer.

1. 60 yards or 100 meters?
2. 100 yards or 100 meters?
3. 110 yards or 100 meters?
4. 880 yards or 800 meters?
5. One mile or 1500 meters?
6. Six miles or 10,000 meters?

45 Name the Game

Almost everyone knows how to play tennis and softball. But there are dozens of other sports and games played by only a limited number of people and not nearly so well known. How many of the six described here do you know?

1. A form of football played with an inflated oval ball on a large rectangular field between two teams of 15 players. The idea is to kick or carry the ball over the opponent's goal. The game is:

A. Rugby
B. Soccer
C. Hurling

2. A goal game that is played on a rectangular field between two teams of ten players using long sticks fitted with triangular pockets. It's:

A. Field hockey
B. Korfball
C. Lacrosse

3. A Scottish game similar to shuffleboard played on ice in which two teams of four players each slide heavy, polished circular stones toward fixed targets at either end of the rink. It's called:

A. Curling
B. Quoits
C. Skeet

4. A game played on horseback by two teams of four players, each of whom is equipped with a long-handled mallet for driving a small wooden ball into the opponent's goal. The sport is:

A. Rugby
B. Polo
C. Cricket

5. A team game played with a bat and ball on a large field having two wickets. Points are scored by means of runs. Well known in England, it's:

A. Cricket
B. Croquet
C. Speedball

6. A court game played with a long-handled racquet in which a shuttlecock is struck back and forth over a high net. The game is:

A. Squash tennis
B. Netball
C. Badminton

46 Origins

Soccer, swimming, and many track and field events go back to the earliest times, and their beginnings are not too well known. But for many other sports, their origins are well documented. Can you match each sport listed below with the country of its origin?

1. Golf	**A.** Canada
2. Basketball	**B.** Ireland
3. Skiing	**C.** Great Britain
4. Badminton	**D.** Sweden
5. Billiards	**E.** United States
6. Ice Hockey	**F.** The Netherlands
7. Gymnastics	**G.** Scotland
8. Handball	**H.** Greece
9. Roller Skating	**I.** India

47 In Brief

If you're a fan of the sports pages and read boxscores, you're familiar with the abbreviated terms that appear in this word list. They're all hidden in the puzzle. Remember, abbreviations only.

avg (average)
bb (base on balls)
era (earned run average)
fc (fielder's choice)
fg (field goal)
grd (ground rule double)
hdle (hurdle)
lob (left on base)
mgr (manager)
mvp (most valuable player)
opp (opponent)
pat (point after touchdown
pct (percentage)
po (putout)
ppg (power play goals)
reb (rebound)
sac (sacrifice)
sb (stolen base)
ss (shortstop)
td (touchdown)
tko (technical knockout)

K	C	H	T	G	S	B	S	S
F	G	R	D	T	B	A	H	P
K	E	R	A	G	C	H	V	P
B	L	P	P	O	K	P	H	G
G	D	K	P	H	V	L	O	B
K	H	R	G	M	G	K	H	B
B	P	O	F	T	T	B	H	G

48 Vocabulary Test

Are the definitions given below true or false? If you don't get at least six correct, you need a new dictionary.

1. In baseball and softball, a "leg hit" is a ground ball the batter beats out for a single.

2. The "neutral zone" in ice hockey is where the timekeeper and scorers sit.

3. A "sissy bar" is a term used in the sport of karting. It's a rail mounted next to the driver's seat that keeps him from sliding to one side when cornering.

4. In football, when you "juke" an opponent, you fake him out of position.

5. Football's "nickel defense" describes an alignment with five defensive backs.

6. Hitters look upon a "fungo bat" as one having great homerun potential.

7. "Ribby" is a word baseball players use for an RBI, a run batted in.

8. In golf, a "sandbagger" is a player who is skilled at getting out of traps.

9. A "vaulting horse" is one trained to leap hurdles and other obstacles.

10. A "pick" is a basketball term used to describe a type of screen play.

49 Soccer Symbols

The official symbols and nicknames for 12 teams of the North American Soccer League are presented here. The names of the cities, states, or areas these teams represent are listed below. Match them up.

1. Detroit
2. Minnesota
3. San Jose
4. Rochester
5. New England
6. Oakland
7. Philadelphia
8. Houston
9. Los Angeles
10. Memphis
11. Seattle
12. Washington

A.

B.

C.

D.

E.

F.

SOUNDERS

G.

H.

I.

J.

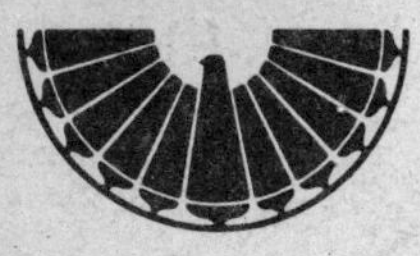

K.

L.

50 Fill In the Blanks

How many of these terms, all derived from the animal kingdom, do you know?

1. A baseball that is livelier than normal is a _ _ _ _ _ _ ball.

2. In golf, a score of one less than par for a hole is a _ _ _ _ _ _.

3. A _ _ _ paddle is a beginner's stroke in swimming.

4. A race car that's difficult to handle at high speeds is said to be _ _ _ _ _ _ _ _ _ _.

5. A swimming stroke that involves a double overarm pull is the _ _ _ _ _ _ _ _ _.

6. A nickname for a football is the _ _ _skin.

7. A punch delivered to the back of the neck is a _ _ _ _ _ _ punch.

8. In skating, a short leap from one skate to the toe of the other, then back to the first, is called a _ _ _ _ _ hop.

9. The disc-shaped target thrown in trapshooting is called a clay _ _ _ _ _ _.

10. In gymnastics, a padded piece of equipment covered in leather that stands on two legs is called a vaulting _ _ _ _ _.

11. On the bar in gymnastics, when you want to skin the _ _ _, you swing your legs up and over your back, so your feet end up pointing toward the floor.

12. If you're not trying your hardest, you're coach may say you're _ _ _ _ _ _ _ _ it.

51 Mark Time

Here's another calendar quiz. Simply arrange the six events listed below in their proper sequence, the earliest first.

A. The Packers meet the Chiefs in Super Bowl I.

B. The Dodgers move from Brooklyn to Los Angeles.

C. America's Gertrude Ederle becomes the first woman to swim the English Channel.

D. The great Pelé makes his debut with the Cosmos of the North American Soccer League.

E. Muhammad Ali (then known as Cassius Clay) knocks out Sonny Liston to win the world's heavyweight boxing championship.

F. Jackie Robinson joins the Brooklyn Dodgers, breaking baseball's color line.

52 Odd One Out

In each of the questions below, your job is to pick the one name that does not belong. It's not difficult to do. Get at least seven right and earn a passing grade.

1. Which one of these cities is not a member of the National Football League?

A. Memphis
B. Atlanta
C. Seattle
D. Tampa

2. Which one of these players never won a scoring title in the North American Soccer League?

A. Giorgio Chinaglia
B. Steve David
C. Pelé
D. Yanko Daucik

3. Which one of these Hall of Fame pitchers never had a no-hitter?

A. Warren Spahn
B. Carl Hubbell
C. Sandy Koufax
D. Lefty Grove

4. Which one of these women tennis players never won the U.S. Open?

A. Evonne Goolagong Cawley
B. Chris Evert Lloyd
C. Virginia Wade
D. Billie Jean King

5. All but one of these is the name of the bowl game; which one?

A. Hula Bowl
B. Sugar Bowl
C. Tangerine Bowl
D. Freedom Bowl

6. Which one of these home-run hitters never hit 50 or more homers in a season?

A. Ralph Kiner
B. Hank Aaron
C. Mickey Mantle
D. Willie Mays

7. Which one of these drivers never won the Indianapolis 500?

A. Ray Harroun
B. Wilbur Shaw
C. A. J. Foyt
D. Jackie Stewart

8. Only one of these teams is currently active in the North American Soccer League. Which one?

A. Oakland Clippers
B. Washington Darts
C. Connecticut Bicentennials
D. Memphis Rogues

9. Which one of these names is misspelled?

A. Rogers Hornsby
B. Martina Navratilova
C. Jack Nicklaus
D. Kareem Abdul-Jabar

10. Which one of these figure skaters did not win an Olympic Gold Medal for the United States?

A. Dorothy Hamill
B. Peggy Fleming
C. Barbara Scott
D. Carol Heiss

11. Which one of these National Football League quarterbacks wear eyeglasses?

A. Bob Griese
B. Bert Jones
C. Jim Zorn
D. Roger Staubach

12. One of these is not an event in women's gymnastics.

A. Uneven parallel bars
B. Flying rings
C. Balance beam
D. Vaulting horse

53 Pick a Number

Sports personalities and their uniform numbers sometimes become closely linked in the public's mind. How many of the "number" questions can you answer?

1. When Reggie Jackson joined the New York Yankees in 1977, he announced that he was going to wear the same number that home-run hero Hank Aaron had also always worn. What number did Reggie choose?

2. What professional basketball player, a dominant force in the game throughout the 1960s and the holder of more scoring records than any other player, had no fear of the number 13?

3. A football center with the Oakland Raiders, an All-Pro selection year in and year out during the 1970s wore uniform number 00. Name him.

4. The New York Yankees have retired more uniform numbers than any other baseball team. The first two they retired were the numbers 3 and 4. Who wore them?

5. If you see a professional football player wearing number 56, you should know immediately what position he plays. Name it.

6. In honor of Jimmy Brown, the ace running back of the Cleveland Browns, several modern-day running backs adopted his number. O. J. Simpson, who broke many of Brown's records, was one of them. What number is it?

7. During his high school years, Rick Barry was a baseball star, and because his hero was Willie Mays he took to wearing Mays' number. Later, as a standout basketball professional, Barry continued to wear it. Name the number.

8. One of the first uniform numbers to become well known was number 77, worn during the 1920s and early 1930s by an outstanding runner for the University of Illinois and later the Chicago Bears. Name him.

9. Baseball catchers have traditionally worn a certain number. Yogi Berra wore it. Bob Boone of the Philadelphia Phillies and Gary Carter of the Montreal Expos wear it. Name it.

54 To the Winner

In 1893, Frederick Arthur, who served as the governor-general of Canada and bore the title Lord Stanley of Preston, donated a huge trophy that was to be awarded to the winner of the championship playoff series in the National Hockey League. Today, the trophy is known as the Stanley Cup. Other sports, of course, have similar championship trophies and awards, although few are as well known as the hockey prize. They're named in the column on the left. Find the appropriate sport for each in the right-hand column.

1.	Vince Lombardi Trophy	**A.**	College football
		B.	Ice Hockey
2.	Lady Byng Trophy	**C.**	Tennis
3.	World Cup	**D.**	Boxing
4.	Ryder Cup	**E.**	Professional football
5.	Davis Cup		
6.	Grey Cup	**F.**	Soccer
7.	Edward J. McNeil Award	**G.**	Basketball
		H.	Baseball
8.	Heisman Trophy	**I.**	Golf
9.	Cy Young Award	**J.**	Canadian professional football
10.	Naismith Trophy		

55 Cage Champs

The scrambled words that make up this quiz are formed from the nicknames of teams that won the championship of the National Basketball Association during the 1970s. If you're a basketball fan, you should have no trouble unscrambling them all.

1. I R S O R W A R
2. K U B S C
3. S I C K K N
4. S T E L L U B
5. T I C E S L C
6. S A R E L K
7. S C O I N S

56 Hidden Number

You must search *only* for five-digit numbers here, not letters or words. The numbers are the seating capacities for various baseball parks and football stadiums. Find each by searching forward, backward, up, down, or diagonally.

52,194 (Atlanta-Fulton County Stadium)
37,741 (Wrigley Field)
55,300 (Shea Stadium)
60,515 (Veterans Stadium)
56,000 (Dodger Stadium)
50,222 (Busch Memorial Stadium)
51,362 (San Diego Stadium)
44,492 (Comiskey Park)
76,713 (Municipal Stadium, Cleveland)
54,226 (Tiger Stadium)
40,762 (Royals Stadium)
52,198 (Milwaukee County Stadium)
54,028 (Yankee Stadium)
50,000 (Oakland Coliseum)
80,020 (Rich Stadium)
56,200 (Riverfront Stadium)
65,101 (Texas Stadium)
56,267 (Lambeau Field)
71,330 (Louisiana Superdome)
76,500 (Giants Stadium)
71,600 (Tampa Stadium)
55,004 (Robert F. Kennedy Stadium)

5	7	6	7	1	3	5	5	0	0	4
4	2	5	5	1	4	7	0	0	5	0
2	5	1	3	5	3	4	6	2	0	7
2	0	0	9	7	4	3	1	5	2	6
6	6	1	5	4	7	9	0	5	0	2
5	9	0	4	0	8	4	5	3	0	0
0	1	9	5	8	2	5	1	0	0	7
0	2	3	2	1	0	3	6	0	5	1
0	0	0	6	5	5	3	0	2	0	6
6	4	7	5	2	2	0	0	5	0	0
5	6	2	6	7	5	8	0	0	2	0

57 Speedsters

Going fast has always fascinated humans. This quiz is based upon notable speed records. With shrewd guesswork, you should be able to answer most of the questions correctly:

1. Nolan Ryan of the California Angels has the fastest fastball among major league pitchers. In 1974, a pitch of Ryan's was timed at:

A. 70.7 m.p.h.
B. 100.9 m.p.h.
C. 120.6 m.p.h.
D. 140.1 m.p.h.

2. Sheila Young of the United States is one of the greatest speed skaters of recent times. In 1976, she established the world record for 500 meters (about ⅓ of a mile). She sped over the distance in:

A. 40.7 (seconds)
B. 1 (minute):50.3 (seconds)
C. 2:09.3
D. 3:31.8

3. The official world speed record on roller skates was set by Giuseppe Cantarella of Italy in 1963. Cantarella attained a speed of:

A. 25.78 m.p.h.
B. 39.78 m.p.h.
C. 56.27 m.p.h.
D. 104.33 m.p.h.

4. The Japanese boast the fastest train service in the world. A regularly scheduled train covers the 99 miles between Osaka and Okayuna at an average speed of:

A. 90.4 m.p.h.
B. 103.3 m.p.h.
C. 148.8 m.p.h.
D. 204.7 m.p.h.

5. On October 23, 1970, Gary Gabelich drove *The Blue Flame* over the Bonneville Salt Flats at the highest speed ever achieved by a wheeled vehicle. He covered a measured mile in 5.829 seconds, a speed of:

A. 394.8 m.p.h.
B. 489.2 m.p.h.
C. 617.6 m.p.h.
D. 1,035.8 m.p.h.

6. The motorcycle speed record was also established at the Bonneville Salt Flats. The year was 1975, the rider was Don Vesco. His speed was:

A. 303.8 m.p.h.
B. 472.7 m.p.h.
C. 623.4 m.p.h.
D. 1,032.2 m.p.h.

7. The fastest recorded speed ever attained on water was by a jet-powered craft in 1967. It was named the *Bluebird,* with Donald Malcolm Campbell at the wheel. He reached a speed of:

A. 141 m.p.h.
C. 212 m.p.h.
C. 328 m.p.h.
D. 501 m.p.h.

8. New Zealand's John Walker established the record for the mile run at Gothenberg, Sweden, on August 12, 1975. Walker was timed at:

A. 3:49.5
B. 3:56.1
C. 3:59.4
D. 4:01.9

9. The bird is the fastest of all animals, and the fastest of all birds is the spine-tailed swift. It has been timed at a speed of:

A. 42.6 m.p.h.
B. 77.9 m.p.h.
C. 106.2 m.p.h.
D. 144.2 m.p.h.

10. When it comes to land animals, the cheetah is the fastest. A female cheetah was once timed at:

A. 39.9 m.p.h.
B. 43.4 m.p.h.
C. 61.1 m.p.h.
D. 87.7 m.p.h.

58 Hoop Stars

Professional basketball stars, unlike players in other sports, often are associated with the colleges each attended. How many of these men and their colleges can you match?

1. Rick Barry	**A.** University of Louisville
2. Larry Bird	**B.** University of Kansas
3. Kareem Abdul-Jabbar	**C.** Louisiana State University
4. Wes Unseld	**D.** University of North Carolina
5. Wilt Chamberlain	**E.** University of Michigan
6. Elvin Hayes	**F.** University of Notre Dame
7. Pete Maravich	**G.** University of Miami
8. Bob McAdoo	**H.** UCLA
9. Rudy Tomjanovich	**I.** University of Houston
10. Adrian Dantley	**J.** Indiana State University

59 Female Firsts

Women have had enormous impact on the world of sports in the past decade or so. Try matching these pioneers with the pioneering effort of each.

1. Janet Guthrie
2. Nancy Lopez
3. Maureen Connolly
4. Pat McCormick
5. Dianne Crump
6. Diana Nyad
7. Kathy Kusner
8. Judy Rankin
9. Marcia Frederick
10. Wilma Rudolph

A. First woman to ride in the Kentucky Derby.

B. First woman to win three gold medals in track and field in one Olympics.

C. First woman golfer to win $100,000 in a season.

D. First woman to win a gold medal in international gymnastics competition.

E. First woman to drive at Indianapolis.

F. First and only diver to win gold medals in two successive Olympics.

G. First woman licensed to ride in a thoroughbred race.

H. First woman to swim nonstop around Manhattan Island.

I. First woman to hold Wimbledon, French, and Australian, and American tennis titles at same time.

J. First woman to win five golf tournaments in a row.

60 Home-Run Heroes

Babe Ruth's name appears on this list. And Lou Gehrig's. And Reggie Jackson's and George Foster's. The list contains the names of 60 players who have led either the American or National League in the number of home runs hit for a season. The *last* names of only 29 of these sluggers appear in the puzzle. How many can you find?

Reggie Jackson
George Foster
Frank Robinson
Graig Nettles
Dock Allen
Bill Melton
Mike Schmidt
Willie Stargell
Johnny Bench
Frank Howard
Harmon Killebrew
Carl Yastrzemski
Tony Conigliaro
Willie McCovey
Hank Aaron
Willie Mays
Ernie Banks
Orlando Cepeda
Roger Maris
Mickey Mantle
Rocky Colavito
Roy Sievers
Larry Doby
Al Rosen
Gus Zernial
Eddie Mathews
Duke Snider
Ted Kluszewski
Hank Sauer
Ralph Kiner
Johnny Mize
Tommy Holmes
Ted Williams
Joe DiMaggio
Hank Greenberg
Junior Stephens
Nick Etten
Rudy York
Jimmy Foxx
Lou Gehrig
Babe Ruth
Bill Nicholson
Mel Ott
Frank Baker

Ty Cobb	Nap Lajoie
George Kelly	Joe Medwick
Walter Berger	Rip Collins
Chuck Klein	Davis Robertson
Heinie Zimmerman	Fred Beck
Harry Lumley	Tom Leach
Hack Wilson	Jim Bottomley
Cy Williams	Bob Meusel

S R U T H R T C E G O G A K
R B E N C H O M F E R S L A
A D N U S L J B R E I Y L N
R O T T A D O K E N O S E B
L B S V A S I N M R E T N A
A Y I J I S B M K N T N M N
J T Y L L E K O A E S S B K
O E N O R A A M S G Y H O S
I K R G S A R I K A G T N N
E F O S T E R K M E C I R S
S I R A M S C A H O D E O B
E L U M L E Y R Y E K M B N
T J I S B T I D R A W O H I
E Z I M O G S V B H C A E L

Answers

1 Match 'Em Up

1.	C	**9.**	N
2.	G	**10.**	K
3.	L	**11.**	O
4.	E	**12.**	H
5.	A	**13.**	F
6.	B	**14.**	I
7.	J	**15.**	D
8.	M		

2 Hidden Words

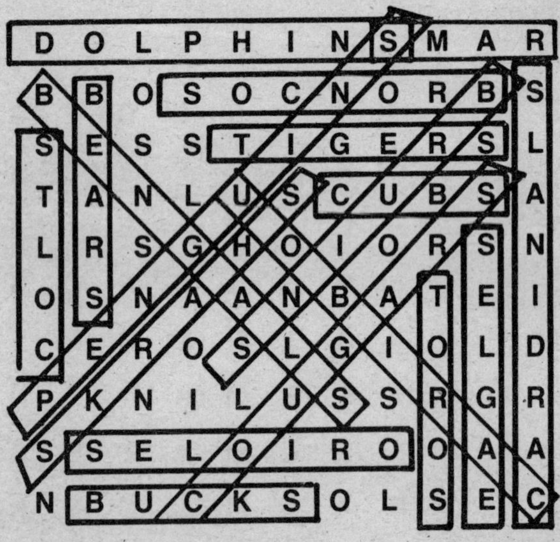

3 What's the Sport?

1. A
2. C
3. B
4. A
5. B (A pacer is a horse in which both feet on one side leave and return to the ground together. With a trotter, diagonal pairs of legs move forward together.)
6. C
7. A (The table used in billiards is pocketless; the balls, solid colors.)
8. C

4 At the Supermarket

1. D
2. E
3. B
4. F
5. I
6. H
7. A
8. G
9. C

5 Playing Around

1. ball
2. mis
3. power
4. maker
5. off
6. squeeze
7. through
8. grandstand

6 Ball Game

1. A softball (3⅞″ in diameter vs. 3″ in diameter).
2. A croquet ball (3⅜″ vs. 2½″).
3. A soccer ball (8⅞″ vs. 8½″).
4. A basketball (9½″ vs. 8½″).
5. A baseball (3″ vs. 2½″).
6. A golf ball (1⅔″ vs. 1½″).

7 You Can't Do That

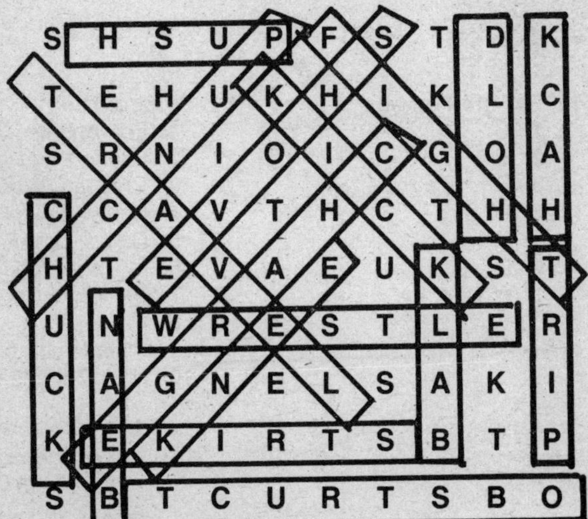

8 Gone Hollywood

1. Alex Karras
2. John Wayne
3. Jim Brown
4. Chuck Connors
5. Joe Namath
6. Burt Reynolds

9 Home Grounds

1. G
2. K
3. M
4. E
5. I
6. C
7. H
8. A
9. L
10. B
11. O
12. D
13. N
14. J
15. F

10 Fact or Fantasy?

1. True
2. True
3. True
4. True
5. False
6. True
7. False
8. False
9. True
10. False
11. False
12. True

11 Scrambled Teams

1. SEATTLE
2. BALTIMORE
3. PITTSBURGH
4. BOSTON
5. CHICAGO
6. MILWAUKEE
7. PHILADELPHIA
8. MONTREAL
9. CLEVELAND
10. HOUSTON

12 For the Famous

1. C
2. E
3. F
4. A
5. G
6. D
7. B

13 Symbol Quiz

1. Los Angeles Rams
2. Green Bay Packers
3. Chicago Bears
4. Buffalo Bills
5. Dallas Cowboys
6. Miami Dolphins
7. Baltimore Colts
8. Minnesota Vikings
9. Philadelphia Eagles
10. New Orleans Saints

14 Sports Galore

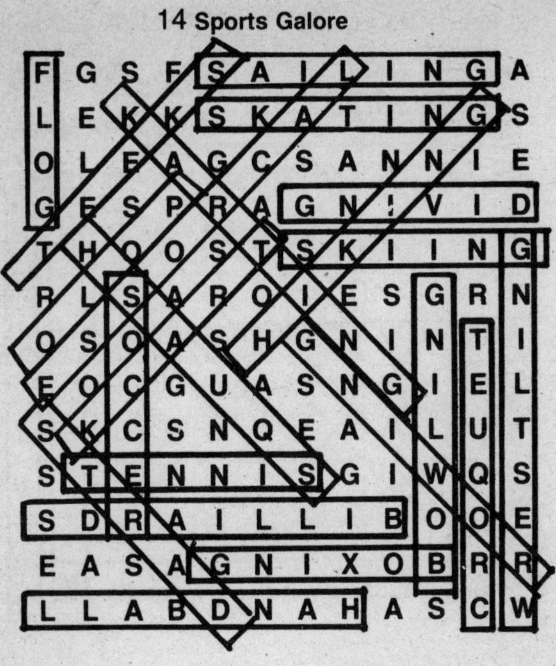

15 **Nicknames—1**

1. C
2. A
3. H
4. G
5. L
6. E
7. J
8. K
9. B
10. D
11. I
12. F

16 **Nicknames—2**

1. D
2. H
3. E
4. C
5. J
6. K
7. F
8. B
9. L
10. I
11. A
12. G

17 Olympic Sites

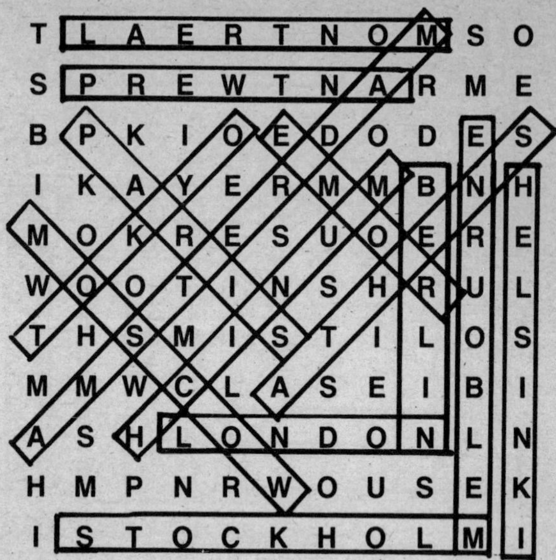

18 Weighty Problems

(Weights listed for each object are maximum weights)

1. Bowling ball (16 lbs.)
   Bowling pin (3 lbs., 10 oz.)
2. Basketball (22 oz.)
   Football (15 oz.)
3. Softball (7 oz.)
   Baseball (5½ oz.)
4. Tennis ball (2 1/16 oz.)
   Golf ball (1⅝ oz.)
5. Soccer ball (18 oz.)
   Volleyball (10 oz.)

19 What's My Name?

1. Jim Thorpe
2. Olga Korbut
3. Lou Gehrig
4. Wilt Chamberlain
5. Harold (Red) Grange

20 Sports-Minded Presidents

1. Franklin Roosevelt
2. Gerald Ford
3. Jimmy Carter
4. Richard Nixon
5. Theodore Roosevelt
6. John Kennedy

21 Flying Baseballs

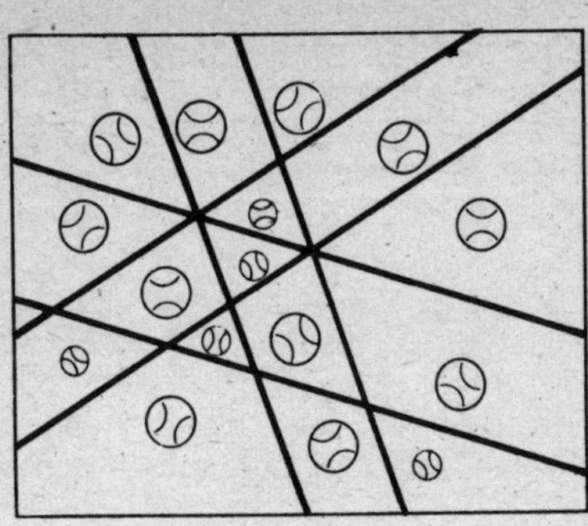

22 Calendar Quiz

1. **B** (1919)
2. **F** (1936)
3. **D** (1954)
4. **C** (1961)
5. **A** (1967)
6. **E** (1972)

23 Skiing Talk

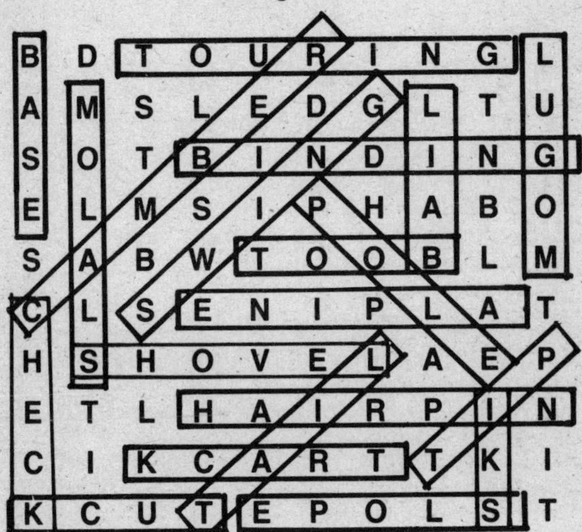

24 When?

1. C
2. D
3. E
4. F
5. A
6. B

25 Kid Stuff

1. A; Joe Nuxhall, a pitcher. He was 15 years old when he joined the Cincinnati Reds in 1944.
2. C; Fred Lynn. He was 23 years old at the time.
3. A; Al Kaline of the Detroit Tigers at the age of 21 in 1955.
4. C
5. C
6. A
7. A; Tracy Austin; she was 12 years old.
8. C
9. B
10. B

26 Spelling Bee

1. javelin
3. mitt
4. apparatus
5. barrel
8. toboggan
11. deuce

27 Well Shod

1. Boxing
2. Soccer
3. Basketball
4. Hiking
5. Football (They're punter's shoes.)
6. Football (Field-goal kickers wear square-tipped shoes.)
7. Track (They're sprinter's shoes.)
8. Running (These are called "training flats.")

28 In Reverse

1. What's another name for Yankee Stadium?
2. How many games does each major league team play in a season?
3. What was the number of games in Joe DiMaggio's hitting streak?
4. On what date was the first night game played?
5. How many home runs did Hank Aaron hit during his career?
6. When was the first World Series played?
7. What is the largest crowd ever to see a major league game? (Cleveland vs. New York, September 12, 1954)
8. What was Dave Parker's estimated salary for the five years beginning in 1979?
9. Which team will win the World Series next year?
10. What did the major league umpires do in 1979?

29 Double-Letter Words

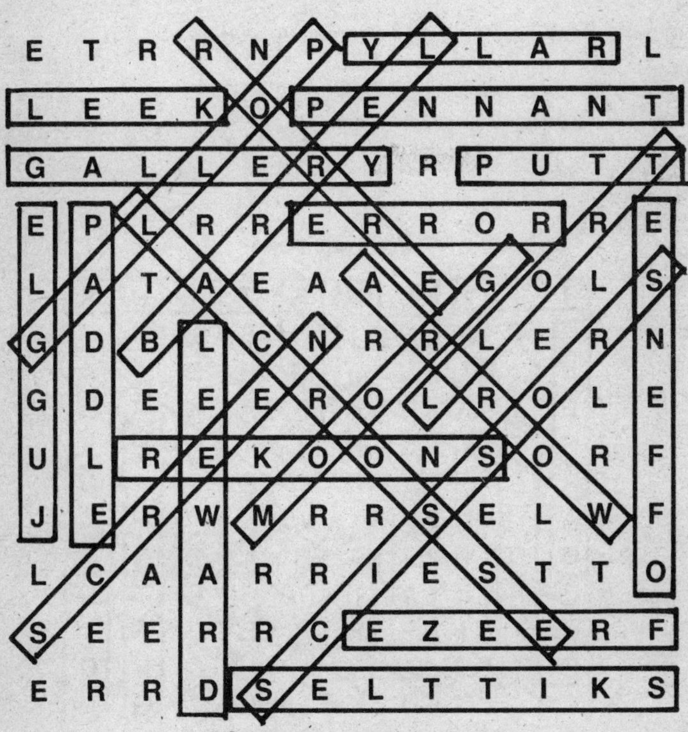

30 Notable Quotes

1. field
2. ain't
3. prayer
4. kissing your sister
5. get going
6. Winning
7. how you play the game
8. one game at a time
9. butterfly, bee
10. the fat lady sings

31 Specialists

S — Safety
CB — Cornerback
LB — Linebacker
DT — Defensive Tackle
DE — Defense End
W — Wide Receiver
OG — Offensive Guard
OT — Offensive Tackle
C — Center
TE — Tight End
Q — Quarterback
RB — Running Back

32 For Short

1. National Football League
2. American Football Conference
3. National Basketball Association
4. North American Soccer League
5. National Collegiate Athletic Association
6. National Hockey League
7. Professional Golfers Association
8. United States Tennis Association
9. Amateur Athletic Union
10. National Invitation Tournament
11. Association of Intercollegiate Athletics for Women
12. National Rifle Association

33 What's the Score?

1. E
2. D
3. I
4. H
5. B
6. C
7. A
8. J
9. G
10. F

34 Women Athletes

1. C
2. C
3. A
4. C
5. A
6. B
7. A
8. B
9. A

35 Well-Equipped

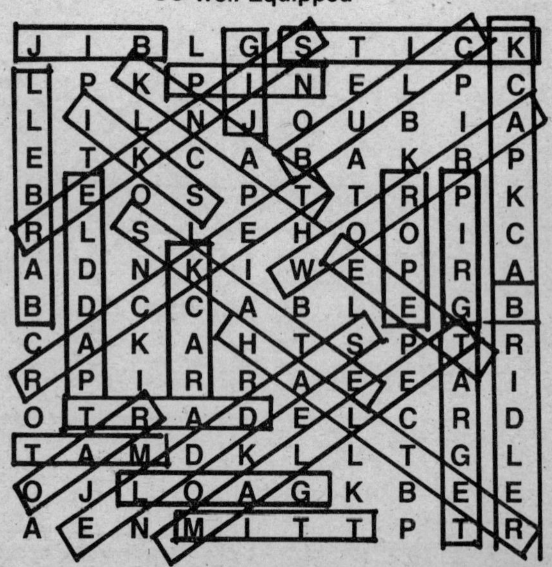

36 Baseball's Best

Photo 1 — **Ralph Kiner**
Photo 2 — **Mel Ott**
Photo 3 — **Babe Ruth**
Photo 4 — **Willie Mays**
Photo 5 — **Ty Cobb**
Photo 6 — **Satchel Paige**
Photo 7 — **Yogi Berra**
Photo 8 — **Mickey Mantle**

37 Tennis Anyone?

1.	D	**6.**	H
2.	F	**7.**	I
3.	J	**8.**	B
4.	G	**9.**	E
5.	A	**10.**	C

38 For the Birds

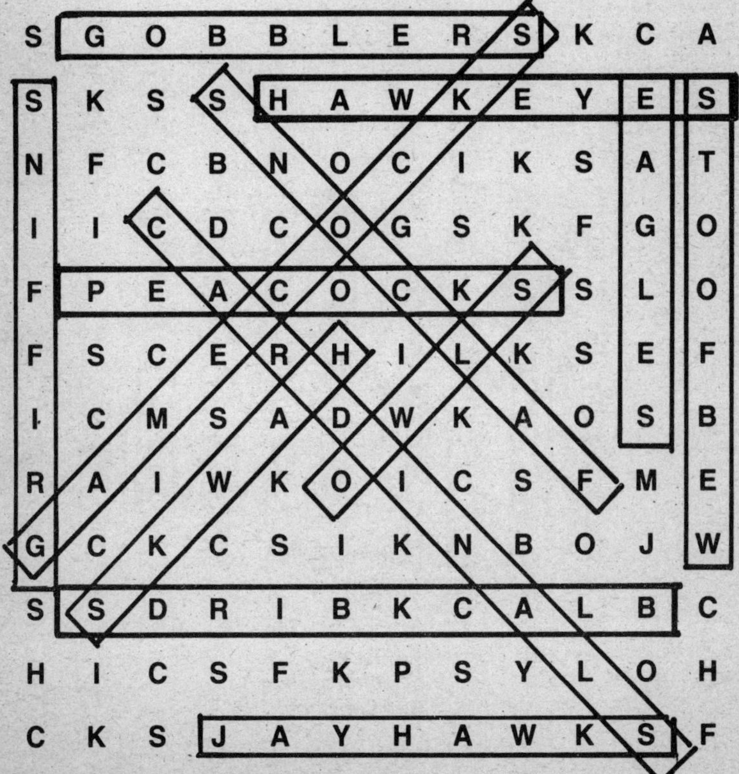

39 Back Talk

1. stop
2. board
3. touch
4. stretch
5. brush
6. come
7. up
8. corner
9. nine
10. door
11. field

40 National Pastime

1. Nolan Ryan (383 in 1973)
2. New York Yankees
3. Cincinnati Reds
4. 1. C
   2. D
   3. B
   4. A
5. Cincinnati Reds
6. Pete Rose
7. Don Larsen
8. D
9. Frank Robinson
10. Willie Mays
11. Hank Aaron
12. Mike Marshall, Los Angeles Dodgers, 1974
13. A
14. Bobby Thomson
15. B

41 Super Quiz

1. C
2. C
3. 1. B
   2. C
   3. A
   4. D
   5. E
4. B
5. A
6. B
7. The New York Jets upset the Baltimore Colts.
8. C

42 Sports Movies

1. *Semi-Tough*
2. *Kansas City Bomber*
3. *One on One*
4. *Rocky*
5. *Brian's Song*
6. *Slap Shot*

43 Gone But Not Forgotten

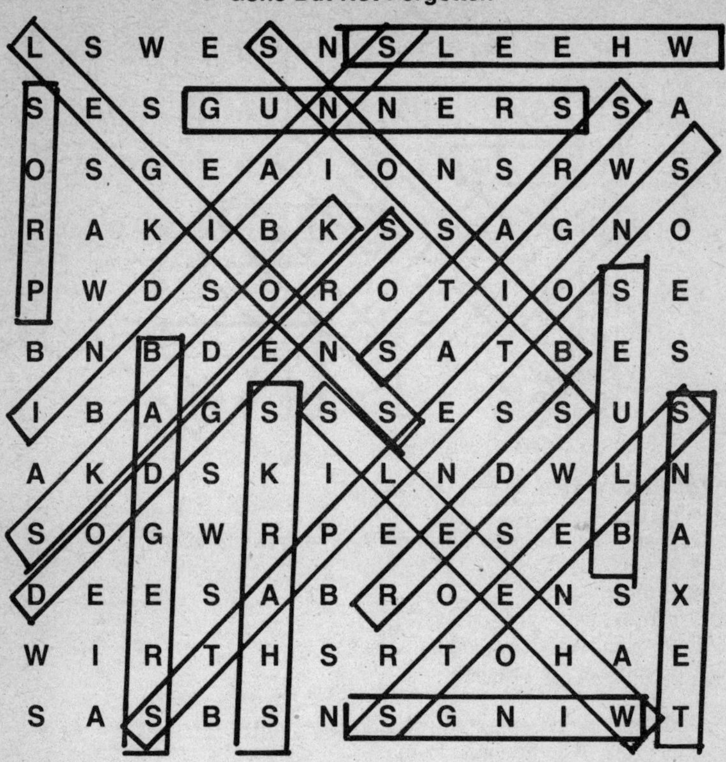

44 Going Metric

1. 100 meters (100 meters = 109.36 yards)
2. 100 yards
3. 110 yards
4. 800 yards
5. One mile
6. 10,000 meters

45 Name the Game

1. A
2. C
3. A
4. B
5. A
6. C

46 Origins

1. G
2. E
3. D
4. I
5. C
6. A
7. H
8. B
9. F

47 In Brief

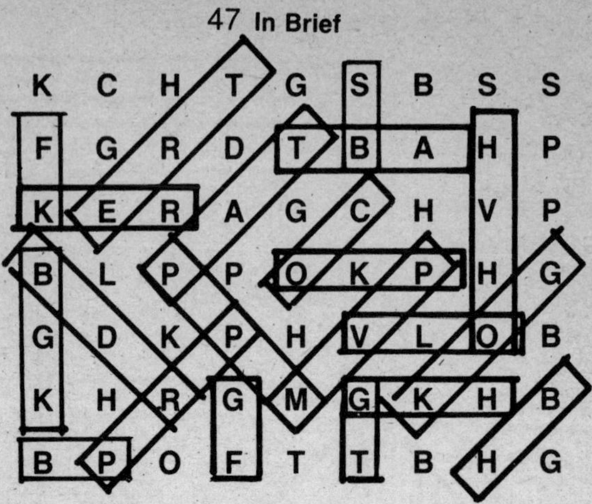

48 Vocabulary Test

1. True
2. False; it's the area between the rink's two blue lines.
3. True
4. True
5. True
6. False; it's a thin-handled bat used in hitting fly balls to the outfielders in practice.
7. True
8. False; it's an opponent who does less than his best in the early stages of competition to make an opponent overconfident.
9. False; it's a piece of gymnastics equipment.
10. True

49 Soccer Symbols

1.	D	**7.**	C
2.	L	**8.**	E
3.	A	**9.**	J
4.	G	**10.**	I
5.	B	**11.**	F
6.	K	**12.**	H

50 Fill in the Blanks

1.	rabbit	**7.**	rabbit
2.	birdie	**8.**	bunny
3.	dog	**9.**	pigeon
4.	squirrelly	**10.**	horse
5.	butterfly	**11.**	cat
6.	pig	**12.**	dogging

51 **Mark Time**

1. C (1926)
2. F (1947)
3. B (1956)
4. E (1964)
5. A (1967)
6. D (1975)

52 **Odd One Out**

1. A
2. C
3. D
4. A
5. D
6. B
7. D
8. D
9. D (It's J-a-b-b-a-r)
10. C
11. A
12. B

53 **Pick a Number**

1. 44
2. Wilt Chamberlain
3. Jim Otto
4. Babe Ruth (3) and Lou Gehrig (4)
5. He's a linebacker. Linebackers are assigned numbers ranging from 50 to 59.
6. 32
7. 24
8. Harold (Red) Grange
9. 8

54 **To the Winner**

1. E
2. B
3. F
4. I
5. C
6. J
7. D
8. A
9. H
10. G

55 Cage Champs

1. WARRIORS
2. BUCKS
3. KNICKS
4. BULLETS
5. CELTICS
6. LAKERS
7. SONICS

56 Hidden Numbers

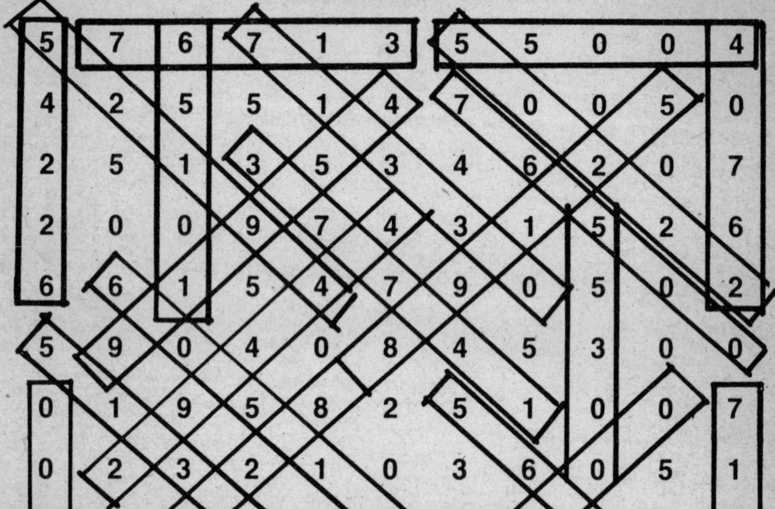

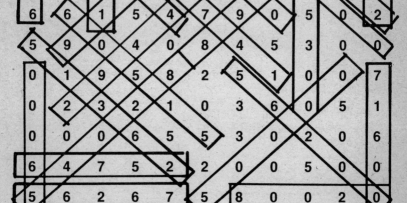

57 Speedsters

1. B
2. A
3. A
4. B
5. C
6. A
7. C
8. A
9. C
10. B

58 Hoop Stars

1. G
2. J
3. H
4. A
5. B
6. I
7. C
8. D
9. E
10. F

59 Female Firsts

1. E
2. J
3. I
4. F
5. A
6. H
7. G
8. C
9. D
10. B

60 Home-Run Heroes

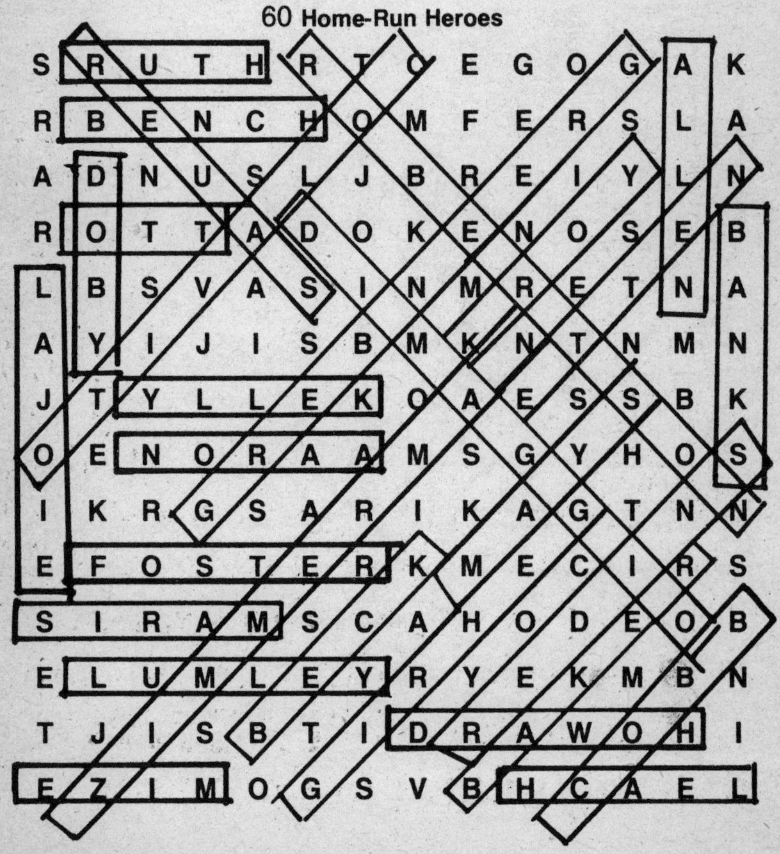